Celebrations

HALLOWE'EN

Hilary Lee-Corbin

Celebrations

Christmas
Easter
Hallowe'en
Harvest

New Year
Hindu Festivals
Jewish Festivals
Muslim Festivals

All words that appear in **bold** are
explained in the glossary on page 46

First published in 1989 by
Wayland (Publishers) Limited
61 Western Road, Hove
East Sussex BN3 1JD, England

British Library Cataloguing in Publication Data
Lee-Corbin, Hilary
   Halloween.
   1. Halloween, – For children
   I. Title   II. Series
   394.2'683

ISBN 1 85210 742 1

Phototypeset by Kalligraphics Ltd, Horley, Surrey

Printed and bound in Italy by G.Canale & C.S.p.A., Turin

Contents

Hallowe'en celebrations

Hallowe'en, on 31 October, is a time for games and fun, for ghost stories and mischief.

It is a very old festival. Long ago, people believed this was the night when witches flew.

Today Hallowe'en is an excuse for having fun. This old picture shows people playing Hallowe'en games.

At first Hallowe'en was known as the Festival of the Dead. That was the name it had long before Christianity came to Britain. Then Christians changed the name to **All Hallows' Eve**, which we now call Hallowe'en. The festival is celebrated on 31 October, the day before **All Saints' Day**.

5

A night of fun and frights

Hallowe'en used to be quite frightening. Many people thought that horrible beasts, as well as witches, walked around on that night. In Wales they were afraid of a ghostly black pig without a tail. In other places, lamps were kept lit all night to keep evil spirits away.

Sometimes people put food on a table for those in their family who had died. They also lit a fire so that the spirits could warm themselves.

Fortune-telling was also part of Hallowe'en. In the past, girls used to stick apple pips on their cheeks. Each pip was meant for a boyfriend. The girls waited for the pips to fall off. When there was only one left, a girl knew which boyfriend she would marry.

Hallowe'en was also a time for bonfires and rough games. In Scotland, children tried to put out each other's bonfires with sticks and stones.

Once upon a time

The festival of Samhain

Many years ago, when the Romans first arrived in Britain, they found people called **Celts** living there. Most Celts were farmers.

The first day of November was the beginning of winter for the Celts, and also the first day of their new year. This was the festival of **Samhain** or 'summer's end'.

Samhain was also a festival of the dead. It was a time when plants were dying. Life would not return until summer.

During Samhain, humans were killed for the gods. The Celts thought the gods would be pleased by this. Food was left out for the dead to eat, as everyone believed ghosts would return on that night. People were frightened and hoped not to meet any ghosts.

➡

Hallow Tide

Hallowe'en did not start out as a Christian festival. The Church turned it into one. Church leaders changed the day when people remember all the saints who have died. They moved it to the same day as the old Samhain, on 1 November. It is called All Saints' Day.

Christians remember the dead at this time of year. In Mexico, sugar skulls like this one are eaten on **All Souls' Day.**

Special services are held in church to honour the memory of the dead.

The 2 November is called All Souls' Day. On this day people remember all Christians who have died.

So Hallowe'en, on 31 October, is the start of two holy days when Christians remember the dead. The old name for this time is **Hallow Tide**, which means Holy Time.

The 'little people'

The Celts thought that the people who lived in Britain before them were the 'little people' who had magic powers. They told tales of little people dancing in magic circles.

Samhain and Midsummer Eve were two important nights for the little people.

The Roman festival for remembering the dead was in October. At the same time Romans also remembered their goddess of trees and fruit. Her name was Pomona. She is the goddess in the centre of this picture.

When the Romans came to Britain, they began to hold these two festivals on the same day as Samhain. This may be why apples are still used in games at Hallowe'en.

Fairy places

Many people were very afraid of being snatched away for ever by fairies. No night was more dangerous than Hallowe'en. If you were snatched away to fairyland, there was only one chance of getting back home. You had to say the right spell at the right place.

However, if you wanted to visit fairyland, there were ways of getting there. It was said that if you went round one special hill in Scotland nine times on Hallowe'en, then a door would open and you would be able to get into fairyland.

Years ago, it was said to be unlucky to be visited by a fairy when moving house. It was even worse luck, though, if fairies were chased away from a place. To stop this happening, people made sure they left out plenty of food for the fairies.

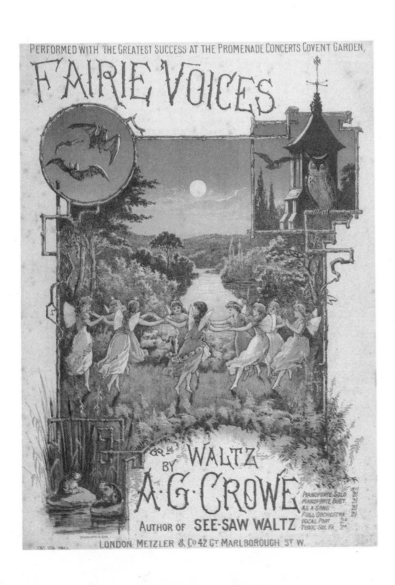

These fairies don't look frightening. But, long ◀ ago, people believed fairies could bring you very bad luck if you were not kind to them.

Witches and spells

When witches walked

Many years ago, nearly everyone was afraid of witches. At Hallowe'en, witches were said to be at their most wicked. Fires were lit to burn them as they flew over on their broomsticks.

Witches were also hunted. In those days, lots of women were taken to bonfires and burned because they were just old or ugly. They were not really witches at all.

In Scotland, people sometimes burned a model of a witch at Hallowe'en. She stood for all the bad things that had happened to the people living there.

LITTLE boys and girls, will you come and rid
With me on my broomstick,—far and wide?
First round the sun, then round the moon,
And we'll light on the steeple, to hear a merry

16

These four women were accused of being witches. If
they were found to be guilty, they were put
to death.

'Leeting' the witches

↑

This woman is being lowered into the water. People believed she would float if she was a witch, or sink if she was not.

One place where people thought that witches met was Malkin Tower in Lancashire, England. The people living nearby carried lighted candles around the tower at Hallowe'en. If the candles stayed lit, the witches' power would vanish. This was called **'leeting'** or lighting the witches. If your candle went out, it was supposed to mean bad luck.

The wood from a rowan tree was believed to keep people safe from witches. One wave of a rowan twig at even the most wicked witch and you would be quite safe!

The poem 'Tam O' Shanter', by the Scottish poet Robert Burns, tells how Tam saw witches dancing in a church. The witches saw him and chased him. He escaped, but his poor horse lost its tail to a witch. Here is Tam watching the witches.

➡️

Magic fire

Hallowe'en was a fire festival. People thought that by lighting fires they would help to make the sun come back to them after winter. Fire also protected them from evil.

At Hallowe'en, Lancashire people used to burn straw and pray for the dead.

Stories about the devil were ▶
told at Hallowe'en.

Holy flames were thought to
guard against evil. Long ago, in
Ireland, a holy fire was lit at
Hallowe'en near the Hill of
Tara. This is where the Irish
kings lived. Every fire in
Ireland was meant to be put out
and lit again from the holy fire.
Only then would people be safe.

Of course, there were very practical reasons for
having fires at this time of year, too. As wintertime
approached, farmers could get rid of dead plants and
fallen leaves by burning them. They also knew that
ash from the fires was very good for the soil and
would help crops to grow in the next season.

21

Hallowe'en torches

This old picture shows people and evil spirits going to meet the devil and witches.

Farmers used to carry torches around their fields at Hallowe'en and say spells to keep their land safe through the winter.

Sometimes people threw stones into a 'hallow fire'. Next day, everyone would go back to the fire. If your stone had not moved, it meant good luck. If your stone was broken or missing it meant bad luck.

Torchlight processions are still held in some places at Hallowe'en.

Husband or wife hunting

Years ago, girls and young men looked forward to Hallowe'en because then they could find out who they would marry.

One way to do this was to bake a cake with a ring, a thimble and a coin in it. If you had the piece with the coin in it, you would be rich. If you found the ring, you would marry soon. The poor thimble finder would never marry.

At Hallowe'en, some girls went into the fields and sowed **hemp seed**. As they sowed the seed, they would say this rhyme: 'Hemp seed I sow, who will my husband be, let him come and mow.' Then they would look over their left shoulder and with any luck they would see the man they would marry!

Many people went to see a fortune-teller at Hallowe'en.

More about getting married

In the days of Queen Victoria (1819–1901), girls would put a piece of lead on an iron spoon. They would melt the lead and then pour it into cold water. The shape of the cold lead would tell the girls what job their future husband would have.

Some girls thought that if you put herbs under your pillow you would dream of the man you were going to marry.

Hallowe'en was once called Nut Crack Night in the north of England. A boy and girl would each put a hazel nut in the fire and think of each other saying:

If he (or she) loves me, pop and fly.
If he (or she) hates me, lie and die.

So the nuts would tell them if they were going to marry or not!

Apples

The apple is the most important of all the fruits and plants connected with Hallowe'en. Apples were once thought to be a link between men and the gods.

Long ago, people believed in an apple land called Avalon where they thought the gods lived.

Apple games have been part of Hallowe'en fun for many years.

The Allan apples of Cornwall, in south west England, were supposed to bring you luck just by eating them. In the Cornish town of Saint Ives, Hallowe'en was called Allan Day, with 'fairy' apples on sale in a special market.

Apples were sometimes used to tell the identity of your future love. People thought you could see the face of your future husband or wife in a mirror if you combed your hair at midnight whilst eating an apple.

The night for naughtiness

Mischief Night

In the past, Hallowe'en was also known as **Mischief Night** in some parts of Britain. It was a night for naughtiness.

In fact, you were allowed to be naughty on May Eve, 30 April, too. So, twice a year, you could smear door knobs with treacle!  Taking doors off their hinges often happened on Mischief Night.

30

Sometimes doors were taken off and thrown into ponds, or taken a long way away.

Often, things got so bad that the police had to be called in. In North America, Hallowe'en naughtiness also got out of hand. There it is called **'trick-or-treat'**. A trick is played on you if you do not hand over a treat.

31

More mischief

If you live in Scotland, you will probably see a lot more mischief than anywhere else in Britain at Hallowe'en.

A good game on Mischief Night was to climb over a roof and pile **turf** into the chimney top. That soon filled the house with smoke!

Years ago, children in Scotland and Ireland enjoyed throwing cabbages and turnips at doors at Hallowe'en time.

Smashing bottles near a window was also fun. People thought their windows had been smashed. If they got angry, they would be 'tricked' far more on the next 'Mischief Night'.

The guisers

'**Guiser**' is short for 'disguiser'. Guisers were young men and women who wore masks or blackened their faces with soot and then asked for money or food on Hallowe'en night.

Sometimes they sang or danced and, if people treated them well, they would not come back for a whole year. They used to sing songs about apples and beer. They were often given beer to drink so that they would go away!

Some guisers looked quite frightening. They blackened their faces or wore masks, they said, to hide them from the dead. Perhaps it was so that people wouldn't know who had been playing tricks on them.

Guising lives on in trick-or-treat. The old-time guisers carried turnip masks and lanterns. These masks link Hallowe'en with Samhain and the masked dances that took place long, long ago. This pumpkin is being made into a lantern.

Magic lanterns

In a Somerset village in southern England the last Thursday in October is 'Punky Night'. This is what Hallowe'en is called there. The punkies are Hallowe'en lanterns made from mangel-wurzels, which are like turnips. They are hollowed out and candles are put inside.

Years ago, 'punkies' were made by the women of the village. One Hallowe'en, when the men had not come home from work in the fields, the women made lanterns and went to look for them.

Today, in Somerset, the children make their own punkies and go around the village singing their song:

It's Punkie Night tonight.
Give us a candle, give us a light,
If you don't, you'll get a fright.

It's Punkie Night tonight.
Adam and Eve, they'd never believe
It's Punkie Night tonight.

Hallowe'en in North America

Early settlers

Some of the first people who crossed the sea and settled in North America came from Britain. These people thought it was wrong to celebrate Hallowe'en as it was a wicked feast. Even Christmas was not really celebrated. So they forgot all about Hallowe'en.

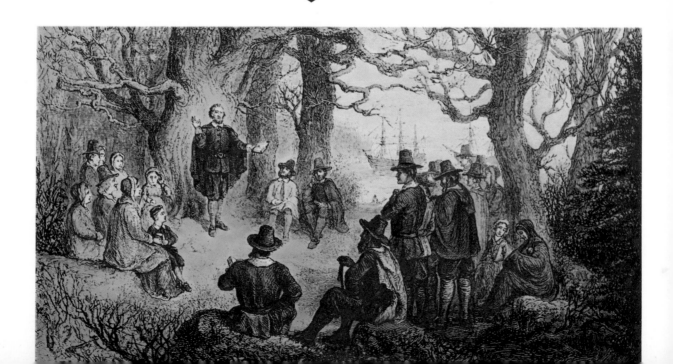

Years later, the Irish and Scots went to America in large numbers. They took Hallowe'en with them. It is still celebrated in the USA and Canada. Many children enjoy trick-or-treating at Hallowe'en. But there are many other games they play at that time, too. One is to look into a stream by lamplight. You are supposed to see who you will marry!

Trick-or-treat

Trick-or-treating is the best part of Hallowe'en for American and Canadian children. People give trick-or-treaters sweets so that they will not have tricks played on them.

Children also make Jack-o'-lanterns for Hallowe'en. These are hollowed-out pumpkins with spooky faces cut into one side of them. A candle is then put inside.

Jack-o'-lanterns got their name from Jack who was so mean he could not get into heaven. As he had played tricks on the devil, he could not even get into hell. So he is still wandering around with his lantern!

This is a stuffed dummy with some Jack-o'-lanterns.

Dressing up is very much part of trick-or-treating. Witches, ghosts and beasts with strange masks are favourites. Today many trick-or-treaters collect money for children in need.

Hallowe'en games

Apple games

The most famous Hallowe'en party games are the ones that use apples. One game is called bob-apple. Fill a bowl or tub half full of water and apples. Then put it on the floor. Next, get everyone at the party in turn to grip an apple with his or her teeth. Everyone has lots of fun, and also gets very wet!

Snap apple is fun as well. You try to get your teeth into an apple which is hanging on a string from a wooden pole.

If you are lucky there will be apple pies and toffee apples at Hallowe'en parties and maybe a Hallowe'en cake. Often these look very spooky with witches, cats and stars on them.

Farewell to Hallowe'en

As we have seen, Hallowe'en is a strange mixture of being frightened and hoping that your wishes will come true.

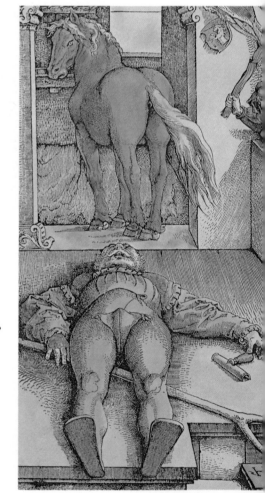

Today the festival may just be fun, but it is easy to see why people of the past believed in it. With Hallowe'en came the dark months of the year when ghosts and witches were supposed to roam. Frightening stories of witches and evil spirits were very much part of Hallowe'en in the past.

44

Over the centuries, from Samhain way back in the past, to trick-or-treat and bobbing for apples nowadays, the fun has taken the place of the fear. Now we dress up and play games, and there is nothing for us to be afraid of.

Glossary

All Hallows' Eve 31 October, the day before All Saints' Day. We usually call this day Hallowe'en now.

All Saints' Day 1 November when Christians remember all the saints who are dead and in heaven.

All Souls' Day 2 November, when Christians remember all Christians who have died.

Celts The people who lived in Britain before the Romans.

Guisers An old word for people who change the way they look by painting their faces, wearing a mask, etc.

Fortune-telling Looking into the future to see what will happen.

Hallowe'en 31 October. It is another way of saying All Hallows' Eve.

Hallow Tide An old name meaning Holy Time.

Hemp seed The seeds of the hemp plant.

Leeting An old word meaning 'lighting'.

Mischief Night A night when people are allowed to play tricks on each other.

Samhain A harvest festival held by Celts at the end of their year, in late October.

Trick-or-treat Games played by North American children who go from house to house asking for a treat, or playing a trick.

Turf Pieces of grass and soil.

Books to read

If you would like to find out more about Hallowe'en, you may like to read these books.

Autumn by Ralph Whitlock (Wayland, 1987)
Hallowe'en, All Souls' and All Saints' by Antony Ewens (Religious and Moral Education Press, 1983).
Highdays and Holidays by Margaret Joy (Faber & Faber, 1981).
Festivals by Jeanne McFarland (Macdonald Educational, 1981)

Index

Acknowledgements

The publisher would like to thank all those who provided pictures on the following pages: Mary Evans Picture Library   4, 5, 8, 12, 13, 15, 16, 19, 22, 26, 27, 38, 39, 42; Sally & Richard Greenhill 11, 23, 35, 36, 40; Outlook Films Ltd. 10; PHOTRI 45; Ronald Sheridan's Photo-Library 44; Malcolm S. Walker 7, 9, 14, 20, 28, 29, 30, 32, 33, 34, 37, 41, 43